Accidency

Accidency

Joel Steven Kuszai

Roof Books
New York

ISBN:978-1-931824-37-1
Library of Congress Catalog Card Number: 2011920511

Cover photograph: "River Dee" by Joseph Kuszai, May 1955.

This book was made possible, in part, with public funds from the
New York State Council on the Arts, a state agency.

Roof Books are distributed by
Small Press Distribution
1341 Seventh Street
Berkeley, CA. 94710-1403
Phone orders: 800-869-7553
www.spdbooks.org

Roof Books are published by
Segue Foundation
300 Bowery
New York, NY10012
seguefoundation.com

Contents

A Miscellany

"Thy art, my gentle Shakespeare, must also enjoy a part."

—Ben Jonson

The Grandiosity of Affection

How small so err
I'll you for greatest praise
How such a poet could you bring forth
 says
it is not enough that through the cloud should break
 I saw birth drowse that Lake
     take steps
 and falls
What should we do but sing praise

    "Our beauties are
   her division
   when she sings

 / quoth he

between rock and rock

                    Amazed to see
                 thinks to frame
           filled with
              broken   A   L   T   A   R
                 A beast
             where sweets compacted lie
             clouded sullen and armed
             of dust from heav'n to hell
             to grave too big horse is to till

lake of brackish waters
further to make room
allarum to my eyes

hue all hues or two
 from state but speech alone
          where to sound thing forgot
          thousand torment thrice three-fold
     to be crossed

face of captive
 before
 and made a Constellation there
shall   advance   flight   in   me

so many deaths
 I live and write

the Sun
remove

the dark
and time's consuming
 couldst think to flee
ease my smart

 it is so with me
oft have I prest
Ah
 Lord
 what a Purchase will that be
      Ah
what bright days were those
foolish Muse
 our murmurings
tread an endless maze
in deep sleep
          calm
as it was bright
 before must descend
at strife

things are busy
in decay
lawfull kindle
upon a wing
was thorn
or more
thirsty
spices grow
the noise
and throng

trees
ROW

folk immodest speeches shun
 the Marrow
by wiser
us up to toil
hope still
sings the note
           in the ear
 conscience rings
this fatal mirror of transgression
 like a tyrant makes my grief game
 wittol think void of sleight

like true   hearts

        live apart

    lives
 If that be all
said I
   made living
their fountains
the hollow seas that roar
a cruel dent
 weight ashes molest

yours ever
      mixt on
expense
 vanished

now
  me thinks
  I am where I began
  all creatures obscure darkness brings
  the dumb shades language spent
                    on the wing
    ours to hold
  perish oft the while
  round beneath it
  sable curls all silver with white
  which freely scornd pretence
  send up holy vapours

Buffalo Inferno

sing
 weep snudge quiet
   scorns increase
softly said
'Dear heart
 soldiers
ready to fight
 some there
think we have a deity
 some
  that refrain'd tears
  have denied
spend the night in sleep

summer's green all girded up in sheaves
lease hath all too short a date

winds heed lest he gets
  love for nought
take my fortunes there
  keep down light
 falsehood did
unframe repent
                    at arms
length to wrest
firm soil win watery
main last Fire
their Truth must try
least of all frown
of shown sad Friends
                    thence by kindle
repelling full fight
sacred virtues protect
they ransom ill
in vein doth cold
blood run   hast hands

descent
        shalt grow
hates to be
created with unprivation
        in cravings
    we have wits to read
    praise to give
we shall enter
        young Cupids
    There
a bed
weep afresh
long since cancelled woe
                he digs out
        the ditch
            while I live
    out their corrupt
my saint   a devil
                did remain
                wrap me in a gown
        dissent
        I think love is rare

you
but one
can every shadow lend

                    your dishevell'd hayre

Anger doth oft to hate retire

permit the basest clouds to ride
 chewed others pens tongue
  more seen
pass men shadows that we see
 even the flowers spring
 vaine empty words
 to brest through the Sun
          Arise
 Thrust
                    sickle

Armor amor shone
Arms were shoulders
sent Arrows cloth-yard
                         nothing
                  larks
    harmoniously

Meer Stranger
      long since dead

  deare to
  flames do work winde
  they ascend
  a nation
vile fruitlesse worke
  loose Retinue staid
the dust
  which please the fates
    their resistless force
labor yields annoy
to grave
       mad-men   stones
  others pin'd the pursuit

          soon they did   strange
an object brought
perfume tinctured   roses
          sunne scatters   light
world's beauty
infant   they were
Nature's family
 this loud brook's incessant fall
          those   whom we
  return
                              to be numb

watering pots give flowers their lives

        every word
        first sight
to bind be flown
                At great doom

      with gracious benefits

           Away
    Take Heed
    where Hee
    crumbled into dust
    Mark here below
       frolic then

      seen either   brows
    more advis'd
    walk as a puritan
    fantastick Ape
    Conquests still are made
    Flames Meteors are
    shews the way
    petulant thing
    hurle ink
    taught tongue to wound
    this place where frosts
    was corn
    tears did drown

3rd Ring Circus

shew that heart makes besides what might have been
things to will this jewell also herself yielded the last
worms be all spent the pools should flow with rain
floods lest unrivall'd loves secure them wake bids
the rash gazer wipe his eye

Knees   crying night

loves to whom
long time
did yield
their aspects
secret glances
till Love raises up
to toil anew
shines with use
good garments worn

                  Brave language
          braver deeds

a soul with too much stay
all company is a weed
an untimely grave
plants such as did their madness
bids the thread be spun

dwells
must
the joy
friend   are

Curling with metaphors
 into minutes
 each
working waves
 that may fetch
 the bounding doe
waves broke
 swift foot
to house unknown

Dear flesh
 while to pray
 learn here
     Dear stream
 dear bank
 where often
their malice
sense
 were to sell

Die single   image
dies with Sweet roses do
 that torrent will devoure
the tillage into Atomes
 winde a rope about
that would rise sight
 muse that warblest amorous
rest the fierce fit with change
still fires vertue sins more
than sins are   Fate
 a brother

 To conclude
 all grief shows false coin
beyond the stars stern war
 blunter poets meet
sweet phrases
 she makes words
 dread to fall stand fast
 the Body can they fly
 head with foot-private amitie

the disease
 that yields
  stores the land
 bodies
as big as thunder
 walks a narrow
 mixt soveraigne
derive
 could spy
  limbe to another
 rebellion
shine brow with sea-bank myrtle sprays

cable
to enforce draw
that what you do may see
melts away
is a puddle
bids fight
kill else
builds a house
which quickly down must go
shot Himself into
apace cool as fast
with ten thousand strings
golden beams
breathe new fire
kisses blow the old
limbs into a thousand
winding curls

"For LZ"

Name comes from the thing
being wise destruction
danger wears plyant
body the act love high
estate neck adore
hid with tresses
hanging down
we view their toil
musing long
scarce well set
those crystal quivers
bravery their rotten smoke
as the Heavens above
Verse be praised

have lost
hast both

the day black Averne
drowned too mighty
raised arms blood
besprent Art
doth again
pomps defaceth sword
broken firebrand cancelled
dismount the highest starre
fainting death engrasped
supply ransom
to provide memory
rosy horses they
dwelt filth forlorn

many paltry
foolish
painted things

piteously with drooping wings stands
a belly under waist
free from lust blind
fortune giddy wheel
sift much but hold soon
her all out am all weak
am link them that to
as dead am with
must take all
'cause GROW burn
down she fell
did bid wed an did
draw but am
do forgive
gentle theif

goodnesse leads him
yet weariness be
wires black wires grow
her mercies cruel restrain
saw the stars drop blood
through deserts
truly said they may take part
borrowed speach
dancing celebrate each
frequent harvest green shade
fountain heir ascent cause
descent best thin array
timber work a winding stair

Is but a Masque
  the servile
drunk
  staggers the way
Is full voices
called out hurled

Is verse enchanted
groves is mark
or Quiver
sweeter than estate

Is this same grief
 within the heart
made wantonnesse
contemplation   Is
when the soul
to the line
accords—

vault
dance
play

Is office
art
news

grounded inward makes the father
lesse to rue
  Where please
Just as I went
None goes that way
complains someone
                  Kill them
 quickening
 Led by a blind
teachit by a bairn
Lest left alone too long
fly what I make
I uncreate
combine bleak palenesse
chalk the doore

Retrofit

Love bade corporeal mold said
"You shall be he who slacked"

Muse smiling did reply
with heat as Death with cold
still pretending

"Lux, your fair fellows
  all may boast as safely vain
  that lasting marble seek
  two that got dispersed
  under a bended moon
  lend her lusty leaf
  fall from a tree
  to will an act
  is long
  but sweet enjoying
  most wits do live
  in glass tell face
  view how half-blowne Cloud
  as winde in consort
  give what a busie
  restles thing
  hunt—"

I acknowledge
in silence how I do despise
Marble
 weep
 for dost cover
 withouten many words
from hazard
a pearle
 a rain-bow

Murder's scarlet robe
white two nights
small price chiming
bell coopelment
shines with deceit
his poore dirtie
mine all symmetrie
can doubt teach
superstition
more sure
less hateful
how the fire in flints
do quiet lie also
fix their reverence
cut (here)
soon as Death's cold hand
cruel in this frame
dissolve rage
for it was to seek thinks
face as mine by love
use their eyes play steel
were & more bright than he
the fire win
those joyes which

Trample his head with prophane phrase
wrastling many a combate
Musick light attend all be while
he turn to clod purling
streams refresh where it bent
thoughts like a brittle bodie
to this school that may learn
burning the first do try
with a sound shall waxe
when wayning right
first consigner those
meaning all day
Rudder bold
began to burnish
Vulture–hopes
a monstrous corrupting
salving amiss Nail'd
to the Center stood proud
unrestrained Appetite—

She blushed 'Red
shame' hangs like
thread wheels spun
magic charms thought
herself endured
She would be allowed
her passions
are let them sing
in my
Shine forth
 but in the dark
of the rose
Short-liv'd low
 don't seem a Starre
Fetter your sex
with make men not
poor souls fear
shade or night
man as fruit of his
cleave my bones
as the will Sin
triumphs still
sunk below
'cuz everyone hath
 one shade

Never let rising approve
you liars Aprill can reuiue
 crystal the air
but curtaine the flowers
garlands gay
 all blasted
 when we unrip
 be grieved
which hast done
 can it the day
shame give physic
my grief did those last
 but (like himself
ashes her last off
rings lose
 simpring all mine age
with Cataracts
 lest if what even now
 knit me that am crumbled
the heape roost
nestle where they estate

mixtures
 compounding Accidents
more
 less
 high
 great
  old

stately height
whose branches met
those blest shades
quench
which as they lay entwinde
building hopes
let not their plot
             Rocks
lee-shores shoals
have thorns
  silver fountains mud
winds do shake
the darling
-cast with Rocks
your mirth
 or passion move
my count wrinkles homeward

        Since then
my God
  let us kiss

                              there's no help
                    early in the yoke are pent

didst so little contribute
as if he had designed
 yet not directly
Swear I was blind
 deny
 if you be wise"
          (she sung
chokt up her breath
day cool calm so bright
 chirping Wood-quire
usurping more strength
than barren insipid
Truth brings forth
or ever as nature did
in breath dull Issue
unswept stone
smeared
          "fel'd him
foyl'd them all

honor still pursue
           I am he
an accessary be not mixe so
my braine excuses quaint words
   trim invention
in ther endlesse webb
steereth with cruelness
 made not as once thought
  also shall might be
witness our false playing
strange shadows
 more pleasing habitation
than the wailing chief I skorne
changing Kings estate to fit
not to live in these times
or may keep form doth show
among wastes of time it is not
all my grief ought to do with me
fit thyself free against I fall
so clean I can till sand in air
come take my love travail
though with one word
night itself undone

as the world serves us
  may serve
air is cold
  sleep is sweetest now
aire was all spice
    applause
  delight
  wonder of our
ayre with perfumes
  our hearts with fire
best thing of our life
our rest
clear wind throws
  dear diamond
let them do their best
    date of age
  or of our death
dew shall weep and fall
night would not leave
  down-right lost
had not left huske
of our joyes in place
sanguine region
masked him from
cost of outworn buried age

Rock of Pride

do not so cruelly divine
what sad ship-wrecked youth
wrought fatal combination
hid soul halation
led pain take verb
web stormy
blastes so sore vally
 or Mountain very
dust dost tread
shake knots way
town from dark abode
shade soft murmure
fall further flight
here he riots
moths still gnaw
my verse my faith
Stay night run not empty
noise suck odours
thence skip the arks
These wonders of love
power your walks crush
unrest toils dangers please
much less give out quarrel
with him for that Act
strike mine eyes so
worship many a sad
own gift good that glance
traduce new rich novice
lavish of his chest
hang content
thought as death

Murth'rer hast kill'd
  Devil wouldst Damn me
now maist change Author's name
often didst with Academick praise
set'st their labouring hands
the vaine pursuit
not climbe those Alpes
full of gall
strong Wine
  youth's Feaver dost enrage
Tulip   restore
be my comfort
end me some unwholesome frozen Age
I am young
  cannot tell
I was once his Enemy
ill-advis'd stubborn I
bared snow
  unbraded gold
forme in table of my heart
I pray in the urn safe rest
  men by knowledge wiser grow

in mee the heate remayning
th' error of my youth they shall discover
 yet I have still the loss
notions in my brain did runne
were as frantick as himself
Three harvests more
serpents resemble
 Thunder thunder
not making
I complain'd
but love unlock'd his quiver
yet cannot see the world
without fence or friend
adverse party is advocate—
 anger comes
 I decline

                                        mercy too
                                    name in books
                              may not rent

        nourisht fame is weak or strong

          past'rall swaines admire
        is ever grave
          rope of sands
            she (war appointed)
          silent eares
            they both comprise
          sweets
            graces
          did tell me roundly
          that I lived
        at heaven's vault
          my bad angel fire
        my good one out
          as show and fell
        a-doting

```
                praise   Name

        both   fruit   order   OW

    lookes grave enough
    a window
    through  grace
    attained with ease
    changed for war
    upon that word
    eat the world's due
by grave
fruit or shade
      at least some bird would trust
    those ravishing sounds
    hide our kisses
    the hated name
    who bears the strong offence's cross
```

Kindle my cold love

kiss the sky
those heaps
cloud me in my way

Whish I flie with angels
 fall with dust
 shadows exprest reached
of course the bank
here enamels everything
How wide is this long pretence
 art my life dissolve the knot
built her amorous spicy nest
 from a sea of light

be happy then
if Nature must
can endure
to write a living line
sweat sayes that fictions
for being fair
a night to have
our compress'd
to what can not refer
whilst I burne
she sings at the souls wrack
on excessive pride
all other brains refuse
most early wit

reading shall inflame
　　short refresh upon the tender green
since each drop of quick store
not suffice our turn
　make shipwrack
borrowed legs
a heavie load to those
but foure words
my words
　be done
canvas
not arras clothe their shame
gloves
　knots the silly snares of pleasure
that makes his Fugitive enjoy
　his brave brother desire

                                        My joy
                                        my life
                                        my crown

  the torment
  of night's untruth   lips of jelly
  your leave can see
  a bairn brocht up in vanatie   like oy
    though the piping shepherd stock
  "O happy fly   visage stern myld
  " quoth I   witlesse wryter
  " eke
  hart   hh psing day
  where drede w never so imprest   violet breh
  heart thrice w'd with Oke
   Brse   so gone
  th m
      heav'nly paradice is th place
  honey tongue of g
  Lillie of Day

To free provisions
  farre above
Adieu
  farewell
earth's impediments
Love is not love
  this the world well knows
art made tongue-tied by authority
  a cunning Painter takes it
so every day
  my troubled head
    to pourpose now then it fell
  likewise back again
(tortur'd with fears) doth fly
doctor-like controlling skill
the world did judge once
need not crave nor cry
quiet to render sight
no one empty-handed
to salute
nothing we use in vain

her naked boy
I follow the coals be quent

Accidency, a hymn

Fugacity of impossible system
acta adorned with fountains
statues agaric thrown emblems
sympathetic symbols
remaining cold particulars
beneath ocular
with greatest possible order
I tumble down again soon my old
words poetry written actions
should issue well-being good
destroyed like animals
infatuous economical uses things
regard minds esprits or rational souls
which produce changes or passage
may be called Appetition
confounds those whose province is action
to quit intimate sayers costly admirable
mechanical structure things
similarly noble actions will attain
rewards in ways which will make
what has happened or happens
 seem inanimate

Nothing walks distinct only
we have seen changes
terror impressess an actual world
shall fall like summer rain
currency symbolized first speaker
etymology finds deadest word
once brilliant picture-language fossil poetry
lime continents infinite masses animalcules
jail-yard relations which though abstract
expresses connexion all matter plenum
our Repudiation wrath rogues
barrows power in swoon or water
most divine among works
should go very warily
reverently We bee secret world
through architecnic ensamples echantillons
suffer or be passive

Love countrymen
 stimulate thy jaded senses
smallest particle matter
escape cusdy that body which pent up
 criticzshem means conception
 appeared like dragons
 instantly mind visits under bridge
 Let us have little algebra
  flat dull people du harmony
Descartes recognized souls cannot impart bodies
  mechanical
are still machines
smallest parts ad infinitum
 ancients observed
 natural change takes place gradually
 homestead ferries
 horses are
 fire she put pan
 be carried about
 no accurate
 between spirit organ
 soul can read itself
 that represented distinctly
 cannot all at once unroll
 everything that enfolded

Act think primarily
explore double meaning
Postulates short   balked
dumb   what sees sharing
path or circuit   through mss.
entire atmosphere if wanted
an immovable vessel
nothing possible we lose ever
substitute something our own
Arch-mechanistic universe
its versatile habit
cascades essentially
intelligent symbols
through which inhabit
symbols workmen feel
few actions privy appearance
sequence or connexion
things which are dispersed
throughout created
poems that are corrupt
three-fourths are nothing but empirics
instance By virtue science
must drink water
out the wooden bowl
poetry not Devil's wine

[*object*] we have shown above that re: she perfect harmony between two realms nature [*object*] she thus that Mamatics speculative orems practical Canons are reduced by analysis Definitions [*object*] City [*object*] how nature present that which she far well time and place sympnoia panta all men recent ages [*object*] city or contract fact [*object*] sensuous fact; immaterial stealth; leaving out limits or bounds things which are limited [*object*] re: are no bounds [*object*] low [*object*] high [*object*] quality life; all [*object*] harmony [*object*] rain [*object*] simple [*object*] compound

Souls act according to laws final causes
through appetitions
 wood iron beauty not explicable
dearer than substance
who are not malcontents
great state
 created or derivative
 products
some motion its own
 postulates
convenience or choice best
raised by means conception rank larger animals
 efficient   stunned
  anim inxication
or quasi-mechanic substitutes
true nectar or who introduces
questionable facts cosmogony
building architect Doubt not
 concatenation due memory alone
 that every created being
 are indifferent modes
 one step nearer
 than any
 expression inwardness

Numerous undulations
air industry
 skill meter myriad more
 figure which came credit G
 knows how on an old rag bunting
  word sculptor who made statues youth
 a public garden
    remember
 good beautiful rests
quadruple or centuple
more manifold meaning
 overlooking that some men
 found internal activities
of simple substances
 might be called perfection
drift within few feet of his cot door
 raising us to know ourselves

re particular changes detail de ce qui
no way explaining how can be altered
quality or internally changed by any
spectacles We are far from
having exhausted significance
of the few symbols we use
can terrible simplicity need that poems should be long
Every word was once a poem in defects
  an emblem On brink waters
  since cannot be by combination
  parts of composition

Thus may be said that we can only
 end all at once; that she say
 since they are compounds
nothing but aggregatum
 exist contingent beings
 since are all representations
one same universe
 from its poems or songs—fearless
 losing the wonder at sleepless
 so constructed
 false all symbols are flexion language
vehicular transitive
 sort muses though origin
eminently trans nature though I do not know a man
whom things so words Bee
impulses figs become grapes whilst eats 'em
With some angels unarmed truth

I read poem which I confide
 an inspiration!
 now my chains are broken
I shall mount above clouds
 opaque airs which I live—striking
 highly-flavoured
detail involves prior contingent things
 an animal soul but made by skill
not machine   each of its parts
compounds respect symbolisent
avec simple plenum
scape-garden   modern house

statues fashion covets
its harvest sown
new hope
old painter
tyrannous eye

Thirty

Two Door Mansion

subject am to her   a force
had suffer nor smart
freedome will tear out the heart
gas the palace
cut down the industrious Bee
whose molten savage answer calls
for object strange cause
any echo cleere forgot

          wild bets
  so Love's oblique may swell
       little hope
from lothe to stay
    love acquit such ingritude
        men are strong or weak
by licence leave

H.H. Silvio the youngest Hee

Author of number   the world
in we it call then I swelt
little hope from
loathe second draught
smally have good will of Silvio
  wanderers still rome

  Let's meet   thought him
 with instant fires
entrey   such a one
  request to try once horror
   no one or none
painted hell
its scalding tectonics impact
melts the ocean down
to a gritty metal abstract
core

Blame Not My Sound

    must sound
            Blame not sound

        Bow
    wow
        Bow
    wow

    our pyres where time emulates
      leape on land farmer   the clowne
    strike they must   the cinders
      suffer a sea-change
    in a turning wing's wind

      Fate does iron wedges drive
    so alternate the designe
      enviously debarrs
    finish according to mind
      little light gives
      lets eate flower
      half hewed unfathered
    that none will dare
      sadde winters wrathe
    season chill
        that God do grant
    know them now
      as envy described them
        left free
    such as they are

Dom Plato's Party

Next green bough to perch which knowes unrest
Map cloud of error grow art proofe against
without tyde or gale reason can this (more
expresse love what you woe an ebbe
being made of steel rust being so much earth
passing forth for knowledge sake
to cut the foaming seas
and let such dangers passe
when the iron blunter grows
selling hours of dross
rash attempt bring him bane
their wonted way
 done blabbing
Death's second self
  seals up rest
 clap their bloody hands
 fright the architects to run
straight its own resemblance find
 a fragrant zodiac
 till that belly swells

O young beauty of the woods

piercing marble stone asunder
show the blood whereof descend
to greater things pretend by saints
  crystal buckets   our wanton kisses
place by common course   trade
 between the earth   root how faire
made their deodands a liar Puck
with glancing wheels drives
the slaughter of Pyrrhus
 still crowning one lets forth
sprite by fate on the just day
heavy   the sky False world
night unknown though break
the lightning-flash Saint
 with accents sweet
reach a mortal wound
 cruel as flame

Death art a Mower too

either our affections doe rebell
bids take delight hard by the crop
must needs (no help) a while toil full of sport
nimbler than a sitting mynde changed our shape
destiny freeze bitter sky was written in nets
that spread the fleecie sheep thunders
violence when frowneth groan when Full
fathom father lies a many bloody deed

The Executioner

therefore
each degree
beginning
tomb

Silvio's speech at the barricades:

Art school is the frame-locked lie
That ungracious pride but fuells
So that knowledge falsely morphs
By Jove to a Bower of shit

Yet kind and artsy Amarillis
A scallop-shell of quiet dignity
A nutbrowne lasse with hands
Trembling with nicotine fury

Be friends whoso list who can
Potentates the lie sold oft
That gold sells love
As poys'nous weedes

Yon blew fame's false fire
Gyde all seking quyete liff
First plow the Ocean
And quest to the extreme

In reply the Mower Damon sings:

Hark
now hear them

Hark
hark

Hark
hark
Harke…

Silvio continues:

Left desperate now approve
Mine eye may be deceived
The forests shook three summers' pride
Mist got sight of our dame

Hecuba with yong daughters all
No man tells cups running the glass
Foes amid secret chambers eke
Numbers languishing

Onely shee bestowes
Lovely dost make the shame
That life was but a flower
How to tell'hem as they flow

Transported by the mode
Offend   must not grutch
All the world were young
Would lead their lives love like

Church court heaven's justice be
Like a lamb he could his looks translate
Sovereign mistress over wrack
A continuall tempest

Art school's reply:

Now true Love
gird the sturdy shores Likely
top-down constructivism
little Reader stay

  bale
    blisse
     solace
      smarte

eloquence cruelty to name equall knots
This beares no brands nor darts
ev'ry living thing   manacled hands
folly and ripe

cowslip-water bathes feet
ills a medicine ever prest
frost then with bow to stalk
tickle point of niceness

Inconstant like the sea
earth took snow-silk
a pure cup of rich Canary-wine
  like Tiresias

The Mower Damon sings:

No
no
no
no
my Deare
let be

No
no
no
no
my Deare
let be

(Repeat)

Silvio's Consolidation of Philosophy

Written to esteem
the common sort
of index thought
your laughter I love
any Flora angry
crime he perplexed
he would explain:
"I be sick with seeing"
"Destroy their being"
"Hearse be vexed"

some end that here
tears be poured out in store
make playn thyn hert
that it be not knotted
that the tulips may have share
for some late fault
on death beds better stone
dear boy
these assemble not
 my lovely boy

        help
    help
   I see it faint

   how shall breath hold out wind tide
   no   it is an ever-fixed mark
    I took pen in hand, wrote:

   quit vain-spent mine gold drum
   sleep should not help harm
   no fire less forged mind love
   doth mark where I rest

   file dream-name your mind balm
   be plaints found may move
   in Time click and sweet spot
   I had not gone hence

Brooklyn Yards

— I'm afraid to admit it
out of the listening —
replacement parts could be a problem
        having spoken
it is moody to descend
salvage what you can

       —*the only way to avoid self-prophecy*

       —*Whaddaya want?*

[*to let go*]

[*to sullen discourse*]

Night in Black Sky

plane sputters in rough fog
    sputters in fog

pure gold saxophone shout
a small girl is standing on a car

Passing, a political poem
    above a ravine
after the accident
the photo's eyes casting downward glances

To whom are our stories but one at a time
The crux of art   And the long lost element
went out into the sunshine
tight, tuned to pitch
water was a theme for her
love a dream of mutual intent

And the news is war
the patrons of the elections
cheered and gave them thumbs down
the sound of siren, tape-loop eternal and
coming after him

Wonder why all the murders aren't connected
the smallest atomic crypt of sense was sealed and cast alight
two lovers stepping over a body crossing the tracks
she held the gun up to [*crossed out*]'s head
why didn't she pull the trigger?
she didn't write a poem
at the word that men will lose
three-thirty in the morning, someplace unknown
what stood before him
in the beer garden
automobiles all lit below
between the dumpster, a brick wall
the retina, the back part of the eye
a jagged cliff between us
and beyond reason

Blazing new paths from school
blips across the night
incorruptible witness
Blued steel

First Cause

fish nibbling at his chin
Flat-back drunk watching stars
hoping to learn handholds
the social formidable

More rain and objects
this tangent for signs of breath
and slaughter
force of natural musk
and the apocalyptic choreography
locked, the final number
its own thought of permanence
continuously active duty to a memory of
                    [crossed-out, war-torn country]
where we made love, no
where we must make
frost biting cold buds
spring seems like it will never come

[crossed-out, nation] tanks rolling over bones

Gestural force of a ghost
seen in the surf
with no heirs
broken everywhere
allowed to wonder, to have been

He beats her
He can't, but I can try
He dreams sirens take mother
He further stated
He has reported that someone
He is older, uncomfortable
He keeps the papers marked
He kicks a skull in the dirt
He spoke of nausea early on
He was arrested
He was front man, price payer
He was transported
He comes looking for her
He doesn't know why
He drank from irrigation pool
He had an idea, a plan or goal
He had built only a moment before
He said for revelation, staggering to his feet
He strums a guitar with an angry chord
He tapping at a portable computer
He telling me he needed the money
He was asked to settle down
He was in an alley all alone, drunk
He was incompatible with
He was an artist
He wrote an essay

In this brilliant bare morning
the last piece of furniture in place
overdose death hidden by silent lights
high in the vertical city
a chariot is adorned with yellow feathers
the engine shakes and quivers
a fear of adding guilt to the world
with speech impaired badly
a bent arm

His skull quickly shattered
a poised unknowing
in what eye is speech
how not to leave footprints

Boneyard darkness distorted guitar
dresser-drawer hidden the fifth grade
jumping, shouting to arms
In umbra, love
in exile
her third floor study
        in mind
in old age
in the back row of the church
the crowd
in the desert — tanks resolve
[*crossed-out, oil company*] forests
in the present narration

Land picture from whose deeds
the infinity of farmhouses
where our toes mingled, you pulled
I heard a voice
launched afoot in boots the street
caught in layered transparencies
reflecting light
less than a playground away
rain in a different dimension
a prisoner counting days with the last piece of a lead pencil
clouds, melting snow
the fight the face fights
the unlessonable auto parts

Live free or die, I thought, suddenly knowing
it would nag me the suspicion
locomare
heave slow slave to rhythm

neither built nor destroyed—

Cows in hillside sunset
she would have to open the door herself
a dried river bed blistering with impermanence
an evil industrial woodland
1000 people
a deposed natural spirit
radiators hissing heat and birds singing at the first blue of day
off her elbow onto the floor

In the subway not any place to sit (let alone write)
who knows if on the main deck of the world
television sets piled
shoot a man square in the face

Painting they spent so long hanging,
[*crossed-out*]'s painting of [*crossed-out, place*];
off to his left was their shared bookshelf
through the barriers
Pebbles of rain
billboard mural of a victorious fist
high on the sinking plane
water hisses thru the wall

Smelled it, couldn't drink
sneaking off from the crowd
So something had happened
evidence of that grew through me
like thrushes, soft sinking riverbank
someone fishing from

Sprinkle to pour
Standing shoulder to the boxcar door
        still warm
she said, I want to know
looking out the window
Grand Central, the Chrysler Building above

Suddenly run out of thoughts
sugar frees as wood
sustains meaning
swallowed or fell
swam over our heads

      take this down
tale of a far-off wanderer

The intoxicant shadow of federalism
The land — The ocean's roar
light by which to sharpen the blade of the sickle
The spokes of the wheel grow through us like grass blades
The steep bank greased
The stone wall is complete
The time to ask The trauma of the night before
The uniform, the siren, the badge, the gun
The unusual position of his head
The absent absolutist wording sweeping
air poisoned by its toxic vapors
The apartment you called home
The exception of the singular
The fallen year's tears
The falling light
The fish swim upside down
The gutteral apocalypse of apology
The way police yell through megaphones into a crowd
The way scribes formed words in the margins of books
The way through wax is fire —

Then withdrew to ask a question
flickers and awaits war
This is how I feel, he said, motioning with his hands, gesturing,
emphasizing the unsteadiness of his fingers.

This was why they were compatable.
 this disaster
I was a wreck, but that was just because I kept thinking of him
Throw a brick through that window there and crush my skull
To [*crossed-out*], it was meant as notice that he was growing tired
inscribed within its walls
give it life like one gives a tatoo life
at the water's edge
mighty gods turned to whisperers
Tonight they would spend talking

A belly of shelter
an island, a bed of sea salt
rests beneath you
unable to shed the light shining
on frosty snow-licked ground
drifting across the lines
a room full of voices

Outside, the sun exploded
sitting at the seashore
the trash in the street
they shot heroin on the other side
while you cower under the light
towards the bathroom

          who can?
who was endless possibility
who was the alleged
who was travelling
whose mountainous clouds
whose sting is a whisper
whose way is lost

Why don't you go back?
why can't we see it?

Wings make wind
houses like coffins in a graveyard
only a memory
climb back into the uncomfortable mouth of the anchor

Words which live – and do something, even doubt

Worrying so much, stop
Would you. Wouldn't you. Why would you. Why wouldn't you.
                                        would I —
would you talk to me?
Wrap my remains in a blanket
writing is

x   have me words
x   heavy on the heels
x   knighted words
x   over the bottle in the
x   st. bernhard
x   true tongue

x   voices in my head

Y – thing renewing the air

Years later
Years of silence

Yelling upstairs to not walk so loudly

Yelt thru screen

You are left unburied
                             left unburied

Afterword

These poems were written over a longer period of time than may typically be the case. Their composition, recomposition, and eventual milling, refinement and reframing as poems took many years.

The silence the publication of these poems ends is the silence that initiated them. A series of personal tragedies that locked up behind private barricades a curse of enforced speechlessness only possible in a community bound by the unspeakable. While these poems may allude to that "atrocity's aristocracy," they do so only by chance, the words here were written, in many cases, before the events that precipitated them. Whatever affect remains is a function of editing and the repurposing of found texts under the aura and auspices of "art."

In the case of "Brooklyn Yards," the found texts are my own writings, juvenalia I discarded as unworkable upon graduating from college. In 1991, while living in New York City and inspired by Jackson Mac Low's *Representative Works*, I began using the computer (MS Word primarily) to scramble and sort the lines of the many hundreds of poems written during my teens and early twenties. A much longer version of "Brooklyn Yards" was composed in 1991-1992 using texts written two years earlier while I was living on the edge of the Southern Pacific rail yards in the Southeast Portland neighborhood known as Brooklyn.

This method of composition would sustain me for more than a decade. I would identify a source text or series of texts, mixing, scrambling or sorting them, producing a block of text composed of phrases from the original but out of order. Often I converted commas to line-breaks before running a macro that would remove the first x-number of characters from the beginning of the new line. Sometimes I repeated this process multiple times. Finally, when I had a block of prose or verse text, sometimes more than a thousand pages long, I would begin cutting, deleting, editing, trimming in a process more like sculpture than writing.

Not knowing where I was going, staring at a block of meaningful language rendered open and blank, I would begin chipping away, looking for the form inside to emerge. Often it would not and the cutting room floor would represent the tattered remains of having nothing to say and the tragedy of not finding it said elsewhere. Other times, a lyrical thread would be found, a narrative fragment expressed in leaps across semantic seams.

For most of the 1990s I produced works using this process, combining and mixing works as various as Joyce's *Ulysses*, the Unibomber's "manifesto," and texts by Jean Luc Nancy. The cornerstone of this practice centered around use of an anthology produced by Jim Powell's English Renaissance Lyric course at Reed College in 1989, which was, in the early 1990s, among the only texts I had in electronic form other than my own. Combined with other sources, "A Miscellany" became the venue, not only for the experimentation with what might be done (and said) using this method, but also as a personal "working out" of the issues that led to needing to work this way to begin with. By the end of the ninth section of "A Miscellany," there is more and more authorial intervention into the text, so that if the opening sections are entirely "found" and re-arranged by the end there is a secondary process of intervention, of writing.

This battle, between editing source text as a surrogate for speech (sanguine reason clipped under duress) and the heroic re-acquisition of speech-making capacity by the end, is for me the central motif of this book. These poems, once composed, underwent a many year process of fine-tuning, as I would often read these poems to myself, in a ritual performance that took a chisel to the edges even while an accrued patina of meaning built up for me around the saying of them.

For years I have inhabited these poems in the performance of that movement, a ritual rebuilding of capacity through mimicry and song. Letting them go now "into the world" is something that has been difficult, for while I can still enact these poems through private recitation, the duration which ends here had at its center a decidedly different view of poetry, one more associated with a poetics of risk or embarrassment—a kind of romantic subjectivity that finds its form even in nature. Not the expression of a self but the discovery of that self everywhere. While the psychic space which engendered these poems is forever lost, it is never far away.

ROOF BOOKS
the best in language since 1976

Arakawa, Gins, Madeline. **Making Dying Illegal**. 224p. $22.95.

Dworkin, Craig, editor. **The Consequence of Innovation: 21st Century Poetics**. 304p. $29.95.

Fodaski, Elizabeth. **Document**. 80p. $13.95

Gordon, Nada. **Scented Rushes**. 104p. $13.95

Guest, Barbara. **Dürer in the Window, Reflexions on Art**.
    Book design by Richard Tuttle. Four color throughout. 80p. $24.95.

Retallack, Joan. **Procedural Elegies/Western Civ Cont/**. 120p. $14.95.

Shaw, Lytle, editor. **Nineteen Lines: A Drawing Center Writing Anthology**. 336p. $24.95

Torres, Edwin. **Yes Thing No Thing**. 128 p. $14.95.

ROOF BOOKS are published by
Segue Foundation
300 Bowery • New York, NY 10012

For a complete list of titles visit our website at
seguefoundation.com

ROOF BOOKS are distributed by
SMALL PRESS DISTRIBUTION
1341 Seventh Street • Berkeley, CA. 94710-1403.
Phone orders: 800-869-7553
spdbooks.org